LIVEWIRE
YOUTH FICTION

Keep it in
the Family

Iris Howden

Published in association with
The Basic Skills Agency

Hodder & Stoughton

Acknowledgements
Illustrations: Chris Rothero/Linden Artists.
Cover: Stuart Williams/Organisation.

Orders: please contact Bookpoint Ltd, 39 Milton Park, Abingdon, Oxon OX14
4TD. Telephone: (44) 01235 400414, Fax: (44) 01235 400454. Lines are open
from 9.00–6.00, Monday to Saturday, with a 24 hour message answering service.
Email address: orders@bookpoint.co.uk

British Library Cataloguing in Publication Data
A catalogue record is available from The British Library

ISBN 0 340 72097 2

First published 1998
Impression number   10 9 8 7 6 5 4 3 2 1
Year   2002 2001 2000 1999 1998

Typeset by Fakenham Photosetting Limited, Fakenham, Norfolk NR21 8NL
Printed in Great Britain for Hodder & Stoughton Educational, a division of
Hodder Headline Plc, 338 Euston Road, London NW1 3BH by Athenaeum Press
Ltd, Gateshead, Tyne & Wear.

Keep it in the Family

Contents

1	A Phone Call	1
2	I Meet my Mother	10
3	Another Phone Call	18
4	I Meet Richie	25
5	I Meet my Father	31
6	The Party	37

1

A Phone Call

I always knew I was adopted.
My mum told me when I was little,
I must have been about six or seven.
'You were a very special baby,' she said.
'We chose you to be our baby.'

My mum had a home catalogue.
She used to buy things from it.
Sheets and towels for the house.
Clothes for me.
She would let me choose
a new dress or a jumper.
I got the idea she had chosen me
in the same way – from a book.

It didn't matter at the time.
It was only when I got older.
My friends would say,
'You're adopted aren't you?'
Or sometimes they'd ask,
'Don't you want to find out
about your real mother?'
To me, my Mum was my real mother.
My Dad was my real father.
I had never known any others.

They adopted me when I was six weeks old.
They couldn't have children of their own.
Mum and Dad were a bit older
than my friends' parents.
They were quiet, kind people.
They gave me everything I wanted.

I had a good, loving home.
I had a job I liked in a local hotel,
and a boyfriend called Mark.
I was quite happy.
Then, one day, I got a phone call.
It was from an agency.
An agency that looked for children
who had been adopted.

The woman on the phone asked my name:
'Janet Stewart? Born 22 April 1980?'
'Yes,' I said. I was puzzled.
I couldn't think who she was.
'We've heard from your natural mother,'
the woman said.
'She wants to meet you.'

I was stunned.
I couldn't answer for a moment.
'There's no need to make up your mind
right away,' the woman went on.
'My name is Meg Jones.
I'll give you my phone number.
It's up to you. Think about it.
If you do want to contact
your natural mother, give me a ring.
I can arrange a meeting.'

'Who was that, dear?' my Mum asked.
I was tempted to say 'No-one,
it was a wrong number.'
But I didn't.
Mum had always brought me up
to be open. To talk things over.
I told her what the woman had said.
Mum didn't seem surprised. She said,
'I thought this might happen one day.
Well, you're 18 now. It's up to you.'

My boyfriend was against the idea.
'Don't do it, Jan,' Mark said.
'Why upset your Mum and Dad?
What good would it do?
I'd leave things the way they are.'

I didn't know what to do.
My parents had been so good to me.
I didn't want to hurt them.
On the other hand I did want to know
what my real mother was like.

I asked my Dad what he thought.
He was in the green-house
potting up his plants.
'Well, Jan,' he said. 'It's your choice.
But you may regret it if you don't
take this chance to meet your mother.
We'll still be here for you.'

2

I Meet my Mother

Mark and I both worked at the Royal Hotel.
I was a receptionist there
and Mark was a trainee manager.
We were both new to the job.
Mark often had to go on training courses.
Not long after I heard about my mother,
Mark was sent on one.
He would be away for a month.

While he was away I rang Meg Jones.
I told her I wanted to meet my mother.
I did it while Mark was away.
I knew he would try to change my mind.
It was something I had to do by myself.

It was all quite easy.
Meg Jones set up a meeting for us
on my day off.
I was to meet my real mother in Newport.
This was a sea-side town not far away.
Meg gave me the name of the hotel.
We were to meet at twelve o'clock
at the Crown Hotel.

I felt very nervous on the train going.
I began to wonder how I'd feel about
my mother. What she'd be like.
I knew nothing about her,
only her name, Stella Harris.
I took a taxi from the station.
I didn't want to be late.

The Crown Hotel was a dump.
It was run down and scruffy.
Not a bit like the smart hotel
where I worked.
Our manager, Mr Khan, would have
had a fit if he'd seen the state of it.
The lounge was empty.

I went into the bar.
There were a few men here.
Salesmen, sorting out their paper work.
A woman sat alone by the window.
She looked up as I came in.
I knew at once this was my mother.
She was very like me.

Stella Harris was about my height.
She had the same kind of hair.
The same eyes. The same nose.
It was like looking at myself
in years to come.
My mother came up to me.
'I'm Stella,' she said. 'You must be Jan.'

She seemed a bit on edge.
She lit a cigarette
and took a deep breath.
'What will you have to drink?' she asked.
'An orange juice, please,' I said.
My mother had a gin and tonic.
We took our drinks and sat down.

Nobody said anything for a while.
We looked at each other.
I knew I was better dressed.
I have to look smart for work.
My mother's suit was old.
Her blouse was not very clean.
Her nail varnish was chipped.
I thought we would go somewhere
else for lunch. Somewhere nicer.
My mother said she wasn't hungry.
I asked the waiter to bring me a sandwich.
My mother asked for another gin.

We began to talk. It seemed strange.
Telling this stranger about my life.
About my parents, about my job,
about my boyfriend, Mark.
'Is he the one?' my mother asked.
I told her we hoped to marry one day.
To run our own small hotel.
'Be quite sure before you marry,' she said.
'I've made two mistakes.'
She pointed to the rings on her finger.
'Twice married, twice divorced.'

I thought about what she'd said
on the way home.
My real mother seemed a sad woman.
Things hadn't turned out well for her.
She lived in one room.
Had a dead end job in an office.
I wondered why she had got in touch.
She didn't seem all that pleased to see me.
She didn't touch me at all.
Didn't say if we would meet again.

It had been a strange day.
Not only had I met my mother.
I now knew who my father was.
It was a shock finding out.
It was someone I knew by name.
My father was David Simms.
He owned a factory in our town.
My mother had worked there,
in the office, when she was young.
They had a brief affair.

David Simms was married at the time.
When Stella found she was having a baby,
she left town.
She put me up for adoption.
That was how my life began.

3

Another Phone Call

I passed my father's factory every day
of my life. The bus went that way.
For the next few days I peered
out of the window. Hoping to see him.
I had no idea what he looked like.
But I knew he must be about 50.
There were cars parked in the yard.
I wondered which one was his.

It began to take over my life.
The need to know what my father was like.

Mr Khan spoke to me quite sharply one day.
'Jan, are you going to answer that phone?
It's been ringing for ages.'
'What? Oh sorry,' I said. 'I was miles away.'
'Keep your mind on the job,' he said.
'Stop day-dreaming about Mark.' He smiled.
'Sorry, Mr Khan,' I said.
He wasn't a bad boss really.

I hadn't missed Mark at all.
I'd had too much on my mind.
When he rang I didn't say anything
about meeting my real mother.
I let him do all the talking.
He told me about his course.
'What have you been doing?' he asked.
'Me? Oh, nothing much,' I said.
'Gina and I might go to a film tonight.'

Gina was my best friend.
She worked in a bank.
We didn't see each other very often.
I worked shift work at the hotel.
That week I was on the early shift.
So I was free in the evening.

We met for a snack first.
I told Gina my news.
'It's funny,' I said. 'Meeting my mother
was like meeting a stranger.
I didn't feel anything for her at all.'
'What was she like?' Gina asked.
'OK,' I said. I didn't want to tell
my friend the truth.
I hadn't really liked her.

'I know who my father is,' I said.
'Who?' Gina was keen to know.
'I can't tell you that.' I told her.
'Are you going to contact him?' Gina asked.
'I don't know,' I lied.

I know I should have waited.
Done it through the agency.
Meg Jones had warned me.
'Don't try to make contact yourself,
it can lead to all kinds of upsets.
The person may be married with a family.
He or she may not want them to know
they had a child years ago.
Leave it to us to set up a meeting.'

But I couldn't wait.
I looked up the number of my father's
firm in the phone book.
I waited till I was in the house alone.
I picked up the phone and dialled the number.
A deep voice answered.
'Hello, David Simms here.'

My hand shook as I held the phone.
'Hello,' I said. 'You don't know me.
My name's Jan.
I believe I'm your daughter.'
'What are you talking about?'
David Simms asked. He sounded angry.
'Is this some kind of a joke?
I haven't got a daughter.'

By now I was shaking with nerves.
I could hardly get the words out.
'Do you remember Stella Harris?' I asked.
'Stella Harris? She used to work for us
years ago,' he said.
'What's she got to do with it?'

'I'm her daughter,' I said.
'She gave me up for adoption as a baby.
I met Stella a few days ago.
She told me you were my father and ...'
'What's your game?' David Simms cut in.
Are you trying to blackmail me?'
And he put the phone down.

That phone call left me hurt and angry.
When Mum came home she saw I was upset.
'What's the matter?' she asked.
'Nothing,' I told her. 'I've got a headache.
I think I'll go and lie down.'
When Mark rang I was short with him.
'I'm not feeling well,' I told him.
'I'll ring you back.'

I lay down on my bed and cried.
What was happening to me?
I seemed to be telling lies
all the time. Keeping secrets.
I hadn't been honest with Gina,
or my parents, or Mark.
Why had my real mother got in touch?
She didn't seem to care for me.
I wished I had never met her.

Mark had been right.
From now on I would let things be.
If my father didn't want to know me
I didn't want to know him.

4

I Meet Richie

Then something happened.
Something that was to change my life.
I met David Simms' son,
my half brother, Richie.
A firm rang up to book a room
in our hotel.
We often let out our large rooms
for meetings.

I took the booking myself.
I wrote down the date and the time.
'And the name of your firm?' I asked
'David Simms and Co.,' the caller said.
'This is Richie Simms speaking.
I'll be running the meeting.'

It was strange that Simms and Co.
had chosen our hotel.
There were plenty of others in town.
Of course, David Simms had no idea
that I worked there.
He wasn't coming to the meeting.
I couldn't wait to meet his son.

When I met Richie I took to him
at once. He was really nice.
If I could have chosen a big brother
I would have chosen one like him.
Richie was about five years older than me.
Not good looking but with a kind face.
He was very friendly.

He seemed to like me too.
He stopped at the reception desk
for a chat after the meeting.
'Thanks for all your help,' he said.
'The meeting went really well.
The lunch was excellent.
We'll use your hotel again.'

He hung about for a while.
'I wonder if you'd like to come out
for a meal sometime?' he said.
I thought about it.
I wouldn't normally go out on a date.
Mark and I were going steady.
But it was too good a chance to miss.
'I'd like that,' I said.
'Great, when are you free?' Richie asked.
We agreed to meet two days later.

It was a good evening.
We hit it off from the start.
Richie and I had a lot in common.
He was very easy to talk to.
It was as if we'd known each other
all our lives.

Richie drove me home.
He parked outside my house.
Then he slid his arm round me.
'When can I see you again,' he said.
I knew I had to tell him the truth.
In case he got the wrong idea.
I took a deep breath and began.
'Richie, this is going to come as a shock.'

When I'd finished I was in tears.
'It's such a mess,' I said.
'Your dad – that is our dad –
seems to think I'm after his money.
All I wanted to do was meet him.
Find out what my real father was like.'

Richie was great.
He did all the right things.
I knew then I could trust him.
He put his arm around me.
Just like a big brother would.
Wiped my tears away.
Then he came up with an idea.

'How would it be if you came
to our house?' he said.
'We could pretend you're my girlfriend.
That way you could meet dad.
Get him on his own. Talk to him.
And my mum wouldn't get hurt.'
It seemed a good plan.

Richie rang me the next day.
He said he would pick me up on Sunday.
I was to have tea with the family.

5

I Meet my Father

Richie's mum, Anne, made me welcome.
She was a really nice woman.
A bit like my own mum.
The last thing I wanted to do
was to hurt her.

At tea time we kept up polite chat,
Richie did most of the talking.
Then, after tea, he said he'd help
his mum do the washing up.
'Take Jan and show her the garden,'
he said to his dad.
David Simms had been very quiet
all through the meal.
I saw him looking at me hard.

As soon as we were outside he said,
'Now then, young lady,
what's your game? I know who you are.
You're so much like Stella to look at.
I believe you are Stella's daughter.
You're the girl who rang me.
I'm not sure you're mine.'

I told him my date of birth.
The few facts Stella had told me.
He looked stunned. Then he said,
'I had no idea Stella was pregnant.
She just went away. Left town.
It was time to end the affair.
It was all over between us.'

'Why have you come here?' he asked.
'My wife knows nothing about it.
Why ruin her life and Richie's?'
'I'd hate to upset your wife,' I told him.
'But I'm afraid Richie knows already.
He helped me set up this meeting.
I'm sorry if I've gone about it
in the wrong way.
Stella did the same thing to me.
I was quite happy until she rang.'

'When she told me about you,
I wanted to meet you too.'
'Well,' my father said. 'It's been a shock.
But in a way it's a nice one.
I always wanted a daughter.
Anne did too.
We wanted to have more children after Richie.
It just didn't happen.'

'I think it's best if we keep our secret.
for the time being.
I've got my position to think of.
I'm well known in this town.
That affair was over long ago.
I've always felt bad about it.
Anne's been a good wife to me.
I don't want her upset.'

Then he said more kindly,
'I'm sorry if you've been hurt
by all this, my dear – it's not your fault.
Stella was always a trouble maker.
Is it too much to ask you to keep
it a secret for a while.
Until I work something out?'

I was beginning to like my father more.
He didn't seem a bad man.
'No,' I said, 'it's for the best.
I don't think we'll hear from Stella again.
I think she was just curious.
She wanted to know how I'd turned out.'

'My boyfriend Mark warned me.
He said it might lead to trouble.
I'm happy now I've met you.
I don't need another father.
I've got two great parents already.
But I would like to keep in touch.
With you and with Richie.
I hope we can be friends.'

6

The Party

It all ended well
Mark came back from his course.
He was glad to be home.
I was pleased to see him
– now things had settled down.
I told him all that had happened.
Everything, except the name of my father.

Then Richie rang.

He had talked his dad into telling Anne
the whole story.

She said she didn't care about the affair.

It had all been so long ago.

She was glad that David had found
his daughter. It was right
that we should keep in touch.

Anne was happy to meet me again.

I took my parents round to their house.

'This is Richie, my half brother,' I told them.

'And this is David, my natural father.'

I was going to call him David.

He could never take the place of my Dad.

Anne and David asked us to keep
our secret in the family.

Only my parents and Mark and Gina
need know that David was my father.

I agreed. Then no-one would get hurt.

We would say that Anne and David
were old friends of the family.

They soon became friends.
I was able to invite them to the party
I was giving.
It was for my parents' silver wedding.
The hotel where I worked
gave me a special rate.
Mr Khan helped me to arrange it.
Mark laid on a special buffet meal.

The room looked lovely.
There were fresh flowers on the tables.
Candles in silver candle sticks.
A huge cake iced in white with silver
leaves on it. On the top it said:
HAPPY 25th WEDDING ANNIVERSARY.

We had champagne to drink.
Then I made a speech.
I was very nervous but I wanted to do it.
I wanted to thank my parents.
For all they had done for me
over the years.
For being so understanding.

'When I was little,' I said.
'My parents told me I was adopted.
They said they had chosen me.
If I had chosen my parents,
I couldn't have chosen better ones.
Let's drink a toast,' I said,
holding up my glass.
'To my parents on their anniversary.
To the best Mum and Dad in the world.'